IT'S A FACT! Real-Life Reads

The World of the

by Ruth Owen

Consultants:

Suzy Gazlay, MA
Recipient, Presidential Award for Excellence in Science Teaching

Jason Christopher Jones, Ph.D.
Japanese Language and Culture Consultant

Ruby Tuesday Books

Published in 2015 by Ruby Tuesday Books Ltd.

Copyright © 2015 Ruby Tuesday Books Ltd.

Editor: Mark J. Sachner
Designer: Emma Randall
Production: John Lingham

Photo Credits:
Alamy: 12–13, 20–21; Corbis: Cover, 17 (top), 23 (bottom), 29; Getty Images: 25; J.T. Vintage/Bridgeman Images: 9; Look and Learn/Bridgeman Images: 5, 14 (bottom), 27; Public Domain: 8, 23 (top), 31; Shutterstock: 4–5 (background), 7, 10–11, 14–15, 16–17 (bottom), 18–19, 22, 24; Superstock: 6, 26.

Library of Congress Control Number: 2013920124

ISBN 978-1-909673-52-6

Printed and published in the United States of America

For further information including rights and permissions requests, please contact our Customer Service Department at 877-337-8577.

CONTENTS

A Battle to the Death

Imagine a bloody battlefield. Thousands of warriors are fighting.

Arrows fly through the air. Sharp spears pierce through armor. The deadly blades of the warriors' swords can slice off an opponent's arm or head with a single blow.

The soldiers are highly skilled. They are brutal and brave, and each man will fight to the death. The warriors are the most fearsome fighters the world has ever known.

They are samurai.

The Warriors of Japan

Samurai were highly trained soldiers who came from Japan.

Around 1,200 years ago, there were many powerful, wealthy men in Japan. These men were known as *daimyos*. They owned land and castles. One daimyo became the *shogun*. He led the country alongside the emperor. The emperor was actually the head of Japan, but he had no real power. It was the shogun and daimyos who truly controlled the country.

The daimyos were often at war. They fought each other to win power and more land. Each daimyo built up an army of samurai to fight for him. From AD 1000 to 1600, these armies fought many battles.

A painting of a Japanese daimyo

From 1600 onward, the daimyos tried to live in peace. Samurai had less fighting to do. Instead, they helped the daimyos run the country. There were samurai in Japan until the late 1800s.

This is Himeji Castle in Japan. Parts of it are nearly 700 years old. The castle was owned by many different daimyos over the centuries.

Life in Japan

During the time of the samurai, people in Japan belonged to different classes.

The top, or upper, class of people were the warrior class. The shogun and the daimyos and their families belonged to this class. So did samurai warriors and their families.

Below the warrior class were lower-class people such as farmers, craftspeople, and merchants. Craftspeople made things, such as clothes and weapons. Merchants bought and sold goods. Some people were so low they didn't belong to any class. This group included butchers, criminals, executioners, actors, and dancers!

To become a samurai warrior, a boy usually had to be born into the warrior class.

This painting shows a samurai on horseback in the 1500s.

This photo shows a samurai in the 1880s.

The Way of the Warrior

The name samurai means "those who serve." A samurai would serve the same ruling family as his **ancestors**.

Samurai followed a set of rules, called **Bushido**. This word means "The Way of the Warrior." According to Bushido, a samurai should be loyal to his daimyo for his whole life. He should follow any order given by his daimyo. He must also fight bravely and be willing to die for the daimyo.

A samurai was rewarded for his loyalty. He was given land by his daimyo.

A samurai would ride into battle for his daimyo, even if he knew he would probably die!

A Samurai Childhood

Samurai children were raised to be brave and not to fear death.

They were taught how to read and write. They also studied Bushido and religion.

Samurai boys began their warrior training as children. A daimyo employed expert teachers to train his young samurai. Boys learned how to shoot arrows from a bow while riding a horse. They also learned how to fight with a spear and sword.

Samurai girls learned some fighting skills, too. Once they were adults, they didn't usually become warriors, though. Samurai women needed fighting skills to defend their homes from enemies.

A jujitsu throw

Samurai learned martial arts such as karate and jujitsu. If a samurai lost all his weapons, he could still fight with his bare hands.

A karate black belt breaks wooden blocks with his hand.

Fighting on Horseback

On the battlefield, samurai often attacked on horseback.

A samurai had to be a good rider. He also had to use weapons while galloping at high speed.

Samurai shot arrows at their enemies using long bows. They practiced this skill by shooting at hats on poles as they galloped past. They also shot at dogs that were trapped in pens.

Samurai on horseback also fought with long spears. Some spears had a pointed blade. They were made for thrusting into an enemy. Others, called **naginata**, had a curved blade. As he galloped by, a samurai could slash at an enemy's body using a naginata.

A naginata spear

A samurai's bow could be 8 feet (2.4 m) long. Here a modern-day rider shows how samurai shot arrows while riding at high speed.

The Samurai Sword

Samurai fought with spears and bows and arrows. Once they were close to an enemy, however, they drew their swords.

A samurai carried a long sword called a **katana**. Old stories say that a katana was so sharp, it could slice through a pile of seven dead bodies in a single blow. A katana's blade had hard steel on the outside and softer steel inside. The soft steel allowed the blade to swoop through the air like a whip. This made the sword hit the victim fast. Then the hard outer steel sliced easily through flesh and bone.

A samurai also carried a short sword called a *wakizashi*. He slept with this shorter sword by his side.

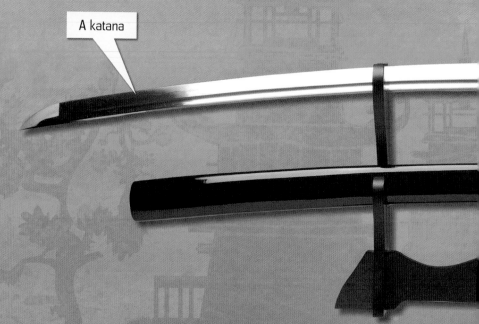

A katana

A samurai from the 1800s

A spear

A katana

A wakizashi

Together, the katana and wakizashi were known as the *daisho*. This means "big and small."

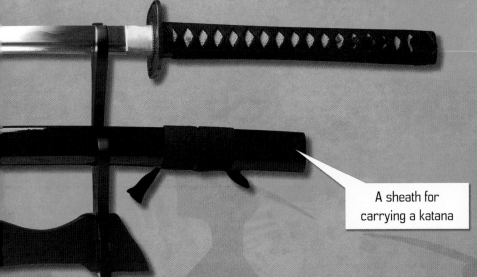

A sheath for carrying a katana

Learning to Sword Fight

Samurai swords were extremely sharp.

It was dangerous for young samurai to train with real swords. A trainee might kill a friend during a practice fight! To avoid this, samurai learned to sword fight using wooden swords.

Samurai also practiced sword fighting by doing *kata*. This was a little like a dance. Samurai practiced cutting and thrusting movements with real swords. They did not touch each other, though.

In battle, a samurai did not carry a shield to protect himself. So a samurai had to learn how to defend his body using only his sword.

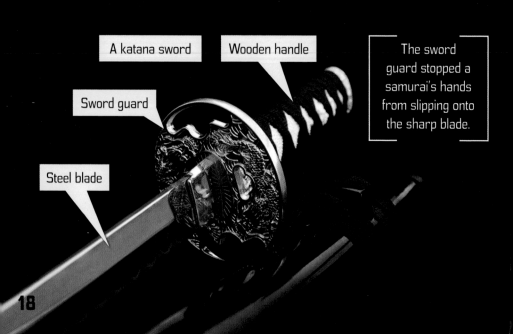

A katana sword

Wooden handle

Sword guard

Steel blade

The sword guard stopped a samurai's hands from slipping onto the sharp blade.

A katana had a long handle. This allowed a samurai to hold it with both hands to get extra power.

Samurai Armor

Samurai fought with deadly weapons.
So, to protect themselves on the battlefield,
warriors wore armor.

Samurai armor was made up of many separate metal
sections. A samurai wore body armor to protect his
chest. He wore an apron of armor to protect his
thighs. He also wore armored sleeves, shoulder
guards, and shin guards. Some of the sections
of armor were made of small pieces
of metal tied together with
silk string.

To protect his head, a
samurai wore a metal
helmet. Sometimes
a samurai wore
an ugly face mask,
too. The mask might
have silver teeth and
a horsehair mustache.
It made a samurai look
terrifying to his enemies.

Dolphin-shaped
helmet

A samurai general might
wear a helmet with buffalo
horns or deer antlers. It
might even be shaped like a
monkey's head or a dolphin.

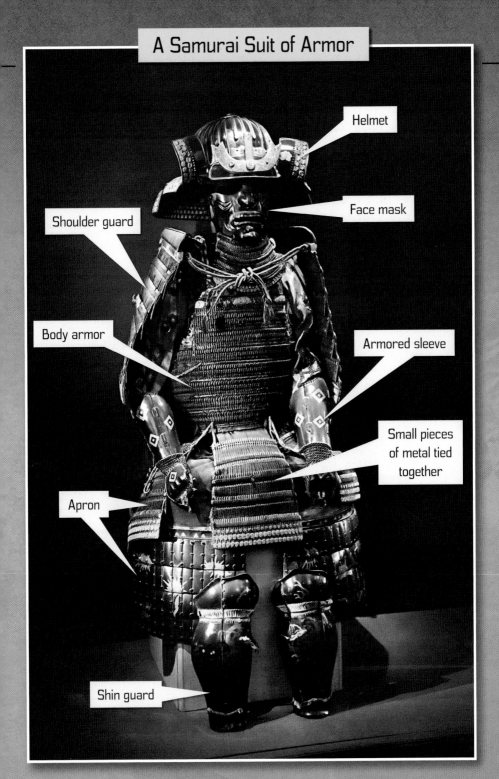

A Samurai Suit of Armor

Helmet

Face mask

Shoulder guard

Body armor

Armored sleeve

Small pieces
of metal tied
together

Apron

Shin guard

A Samurai's Day Off

A samurai was usually fully trained by the time he was 22 years old. Then he was ready for his daimyo to order him into battle.

When a samurai wasn't at war, he still lived by the rules of Bushido. In everyday life, a samurai had to be polite and kind to other people in the warrior class. He should never cheat, show off, overeat, or get drunk.

Samurai spent some of their spare time training. They also had many hobbies. Samurai studied stories of past warriors and battles. They wrote poems, played board games, and painted pictures with ink. Some liked to do gardening. Samurai also played a game called *kemari* that was a little like soccer.

A Japanese garden made from rocks and gravel

This Japanese ink painting is more than 500 years old.

Kemari was played with a deerskin ball. Players wore
black hats, silk robes, and hard clogs on their feet.

Going to War

When it was time for a daimyo to go to war, his samurai were ready.

A daimyo's army might contain 50,000 men. The army included thousands of samurai. It also included farmers and other **peasants** who worked for the daimyo. Some peasants fought alongside the samurai. Others looked after the horses or carried supplies, such as weapons and food.

Before setting off to war, samurai warriors ate a special meal. They ate dried chestnuts, seaweed, and a type of shellfish called abalone. They also drank *sake*, which is wine made from rice.

The samurai put on their armor. Some warriors mounted their horses. Others were on foot. Then the army marched off to do battle.

Seaweed

Dried chestnuts

Abalone

These people are taking part in a reconstruction. They are acting out a samurai army marching to war.

On the Battlefield

On the battlefield, two samurai armies faced each other. Their daimyos watched the action and gave orders.

A samurai was proud to be first into battle. He might ride at high speed toward the enemy or attack on foot. The samurai and peasant foot soldiers attacked each other with arrows and spears. In the 1500s, samurai armies also began to use guns. The battlefield would be cloudy with smoke from the guns. Once the two armies clashed up close, samurai fought with their swords.

This photo from a movie shows samurai archers shooting arrows.

Sometimes two important samurai might meet on the battlefield. Then they would fight one on one. No other warrior would help or disturb them.

Two samurai fight with katanas.

The Final Battle

A sword fight between two samurai was a fight to the death.

Each warrior fought bravely, stabbing and slicing at his opponent. Finally, badly injured, one warrior would fall to the ground.
The winning samurai then ended the fight. Using his short wakizashi sword, he cut off his opponent's head. The winner then presented the head to his daimyo after the battle.

On a good day, a samurai might win many heads. Proudly he would leave the battlefield to fight another day.

If the fighting went badly, however, a samurai might lose his own head. He would face death without fear, though. To die in battle was the best death any samurai could wish for.

A samurai burned perfumed oil in his helmet before a battle. This made sure that if his head was cut off, his hair would smell good!

Glossary

ancestor (AN-sess-tur)
A relative who lived a long time ago.
For example, your great-grandparents and
great-great-grandparents are your ancestors.

Bushido (BOO-shee-doh)
A code, or set of rules, that samurai lived by.
Bushido described the way samurai should
behave on the battlefield and in everyday life.
Bushido means "The Way of the Warrior."

daimyo (DIME-yoh)
A powerful, wealthy lord in Japan.

katana (kuh-TAH-nuh)
A long sword with a curved steel blade that
was extremely sharp. Katanas were used by
samurai warriors.

naginata (nah-GEE-nah-tah)
A long spear with a curved blade made
for slashing.

peasant (PEZ-uhnt)
A lower class person who was often uneducated and did work such as farming. Peasants were usually poor.

shogun (SHOH-guhn)
A wealthy lord, or daimyo, who ruled Japan alongside the emperor. Throughout Japan's history, shoguns gained power in different ways. Some were chosen by the emperor. Others came to power by winning wars.

Index

Read More

Macdonald, Fiona. *You Wouldn't Want to Be a Samurai!* Danbury, CT: Franklin Watts (2009).

Murrell, Deborah. *Samurai (QEB Warriors)*. Mankato, MN: Black Rabbit Books (2009).

Learn More Online

To learn more about samurai warriors, go to
www.rubytuesdaybooks.com/samurai